BEDTIME MATHS

for girls
1 - 5

You can count on me

Anna Maledon

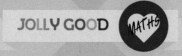

FROM GROUND ZERO TO MATHS HERO WITH

JOLLY GOOD MATHS

Written and designed by Anna Maledon
First published in 2023 by Magical Book
Copyright ©2023 by Anna Maledon

ISBN 978-83-66294-46-2 (paperback)

ISBN 978-83-66294-47-9 (ebook)

ISBN 978-83-66294-48-6 (hardback)

This book didn't travel a long distance to reach you. This book was printed by your local printer.

Thank you for supporting your local community and for looking after the environment.

Magical Books

Magical Books

BEDTIME MATHS
for girls
and boys
1 - 5

Anna ~~Maledon~~

by Eliza
and Piggisha

I love numbers!

I love counting!

And we totally made this awesome book without any help whatsoever from Anna.

Yeah... like totally independently...

i love you

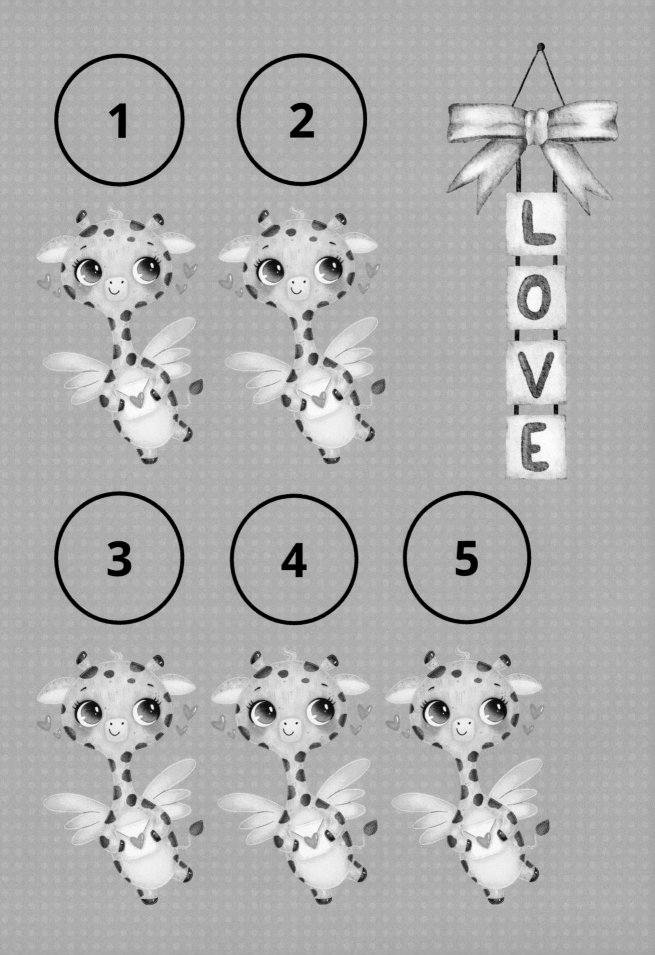

I love you

You can always count on me

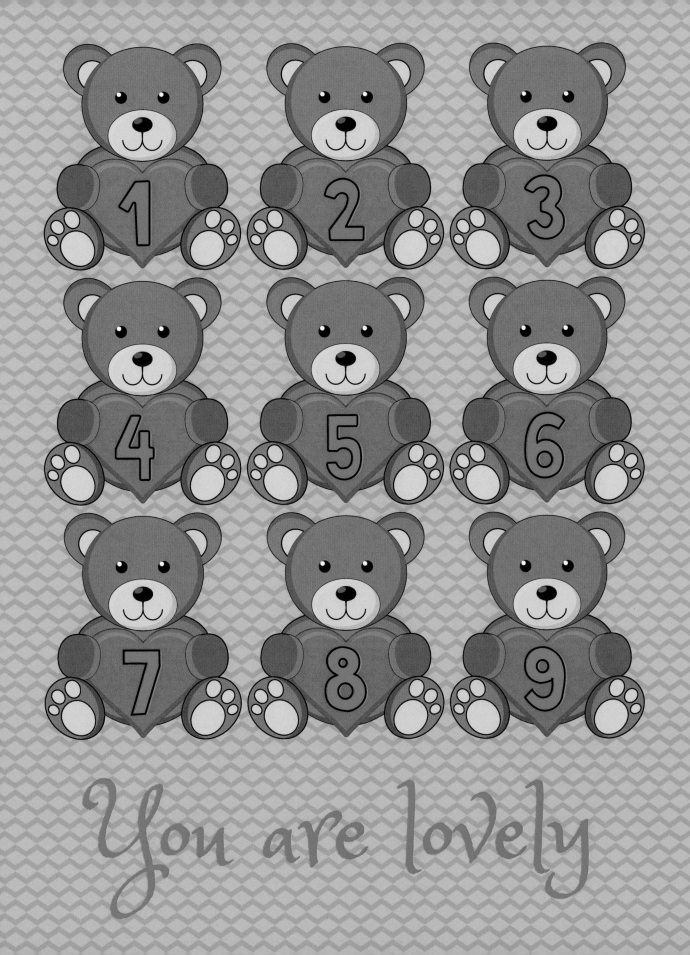

You are lovely

1 My Love

2

3

4

5

6

7

8

9

10

You Rock my World

I love you
to the
moon and
back

I LOVE
you
MAMA

you are so sweet

I am loved

LOVE

LOVE YOU

①
③
②
4

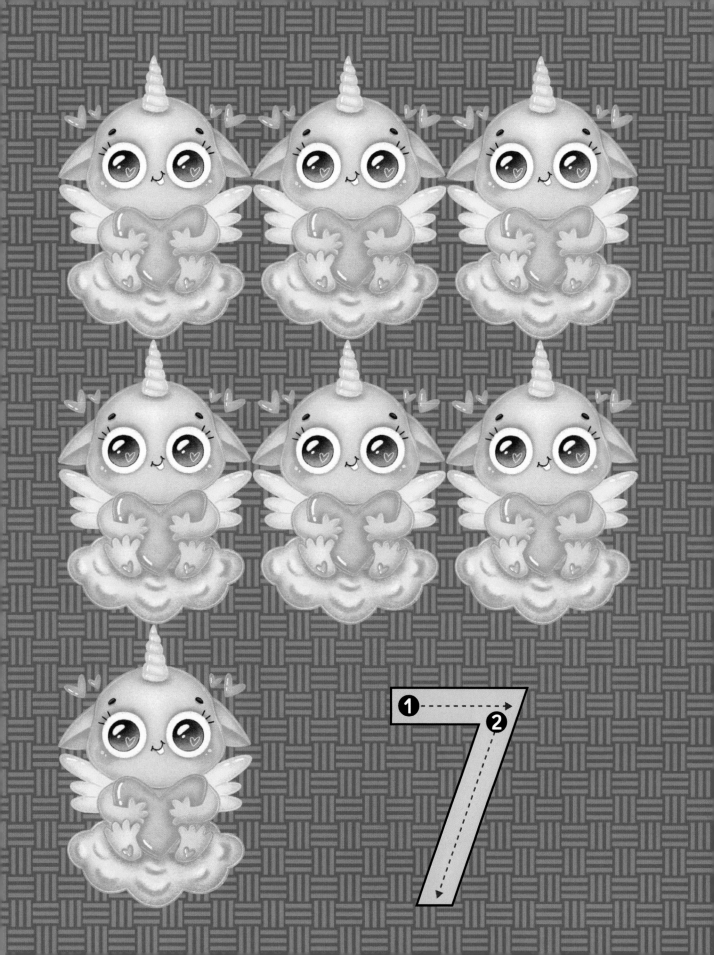

I hope you loved the book!

Please, help other readers by leaving a review.

Thank you!

Shhh... it's time to sleep

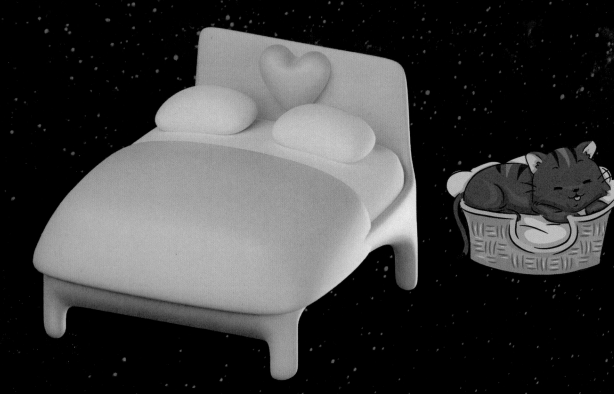

Now it's time to count the sheep

1, 2, 3.... I'm falling asleep

Made in the USA
Coppell, TX
09 June 2023